C0-BIK-572

HAMILTON MEDIA CENTER
4119 DUPONT AVE. NO.
MINNEAPOLIS, MN 55412

A look at
the ENVIRONMENT

Lerner Awareness Series

A look at the ENVIRONMENT

photographs by Maria S. Forrai

text by Margaret Sanford Pursell

foreword by Morris K. Udall

Lerner Publications Company, Minneapolis

The publisher wishes to thank the Federal Reserve Bank of Minneapolis and the University of Minnesota Institute of Agriculture, Department of Food Science and Nutrition, for their cooperation in the preparation of this book.

The camera used was a single-lens reflex Bronica, 2¼" x 2¼" negatives. The text is set in 18 point Baskerville, and the book paper is 80# Black-and-White Gloss Enamel.

LIBRARY OF CONGRESS CATALOGING IN PUBLICATION DATA

Forrai, Maria S.
 A look at the environment.

 (Lerner Awareness Series)
 SUMMARY: Text and photographs explain the importance of a balanced environment, the disturbance to nature caused by cities, and steps we can take to improve our surroundings.

 1. Human ecology—Pictorial works—Juvenile literature. [1. Human ecology. 2. Ecology] I. Pursell, Margaret Sanford. II. Title.

GF48.F67 1976   301.31   75-38465
ISBN 0-8225-1302-1

Copyright © 1976 by Lerner Publications Company

All rights reserved. International copyright secured. No part of this book may be reproduced in any form whatsoever without permission in writing from the publisher except for the inclusion of brief quotations in an acknowledged review.

Published simultaneously in Canada by J. M. Dent & Sons (Canada) Ltd., Don Mills, Ontario

Manufactured in the United States of America

International Standard Book Number: 0-8225-1302-1
Library of Congress Catalog Card Number: 75-38465

Morris Udall talks about the Environment...

What kind of world will you inherit?

Will there be clean water to drink and swim in? Clean air to breathe? Forests for hiking and camping? Enough fertile fields to feed everyone?

These are the questions we speak of when we discuss "the environment." They aren't easy questions to answer, because assuring a clean and healthy environment requires changing old and comfortable habits. It takes hard work, and it takes a lot of money.

This book illustrates some of the things that make up our environment, and some of the things we are doing to improve it. It is an important subject— *the* most important subject, really. Because we only have one world, and we can't afford to waste it.

Member, U.S. House of Representatives
Chairman, Subcommittee on Energy &
the Environment

The world around you is called your environment. To a great extent, your environment shapes your life.

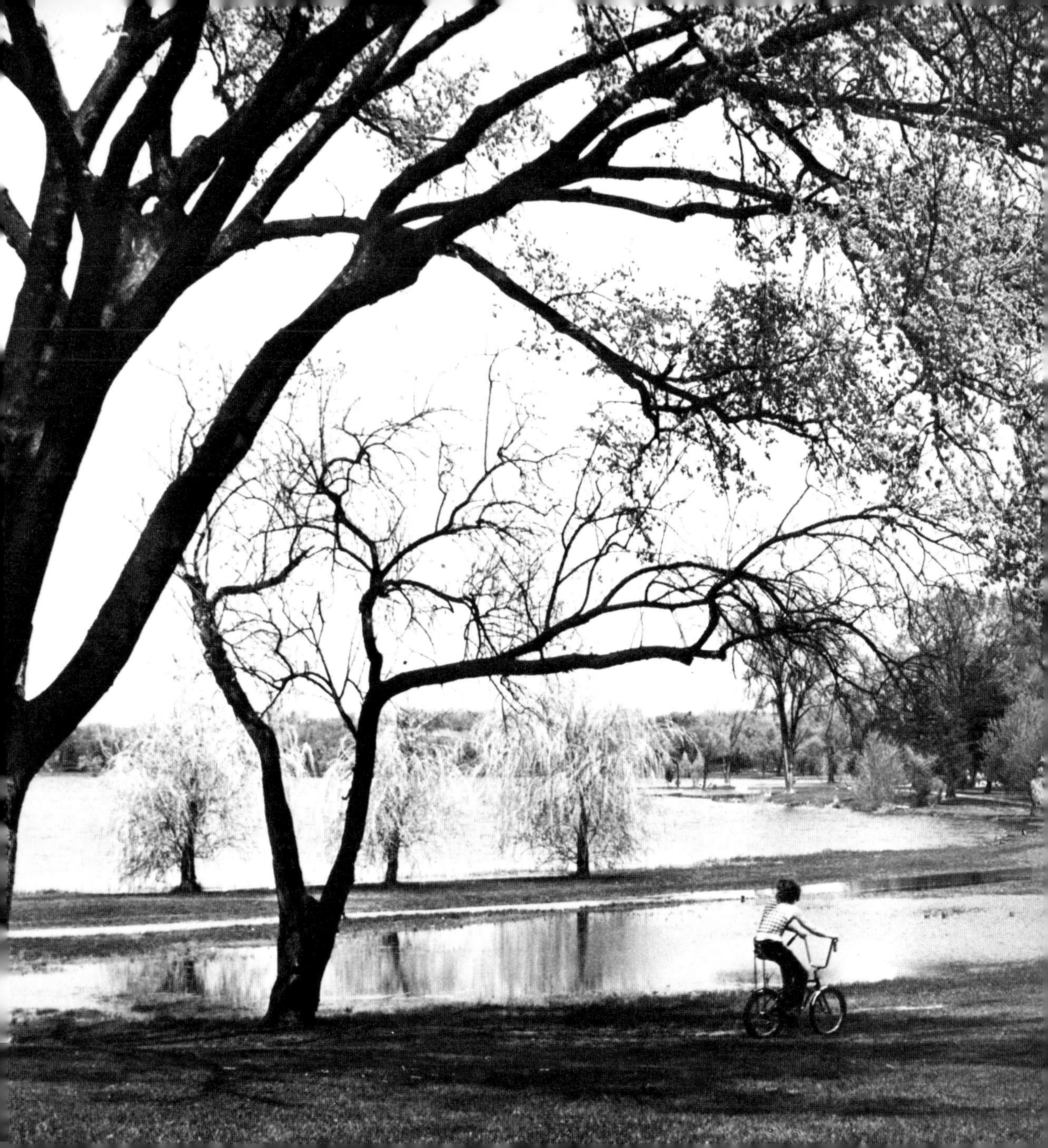

Your environment is made up of everything that you see around you. It includes trees and buildings, hillsides and roads, animals and other people. Some things that you *can't* see are also part of your environment— the air you breathe, fish swimming in a lake, and minerals buried deep in the earth.

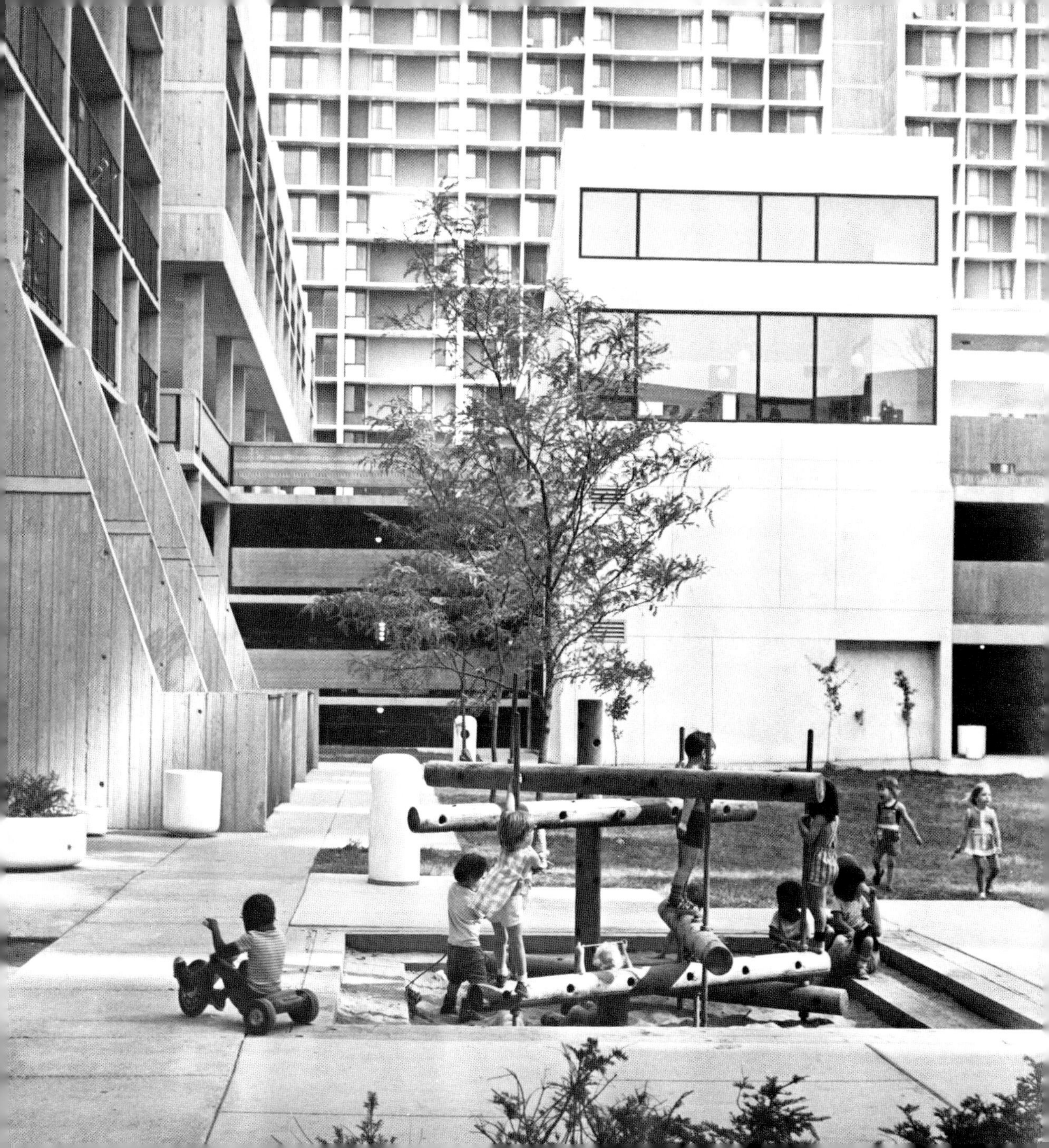

In a natural environment, every living thing has a special part to play. Plants provide animals with oxygen and a source of food. Some animals become food for other animals. And when plants and animals die, they become part of the soil so that more plants can grow.

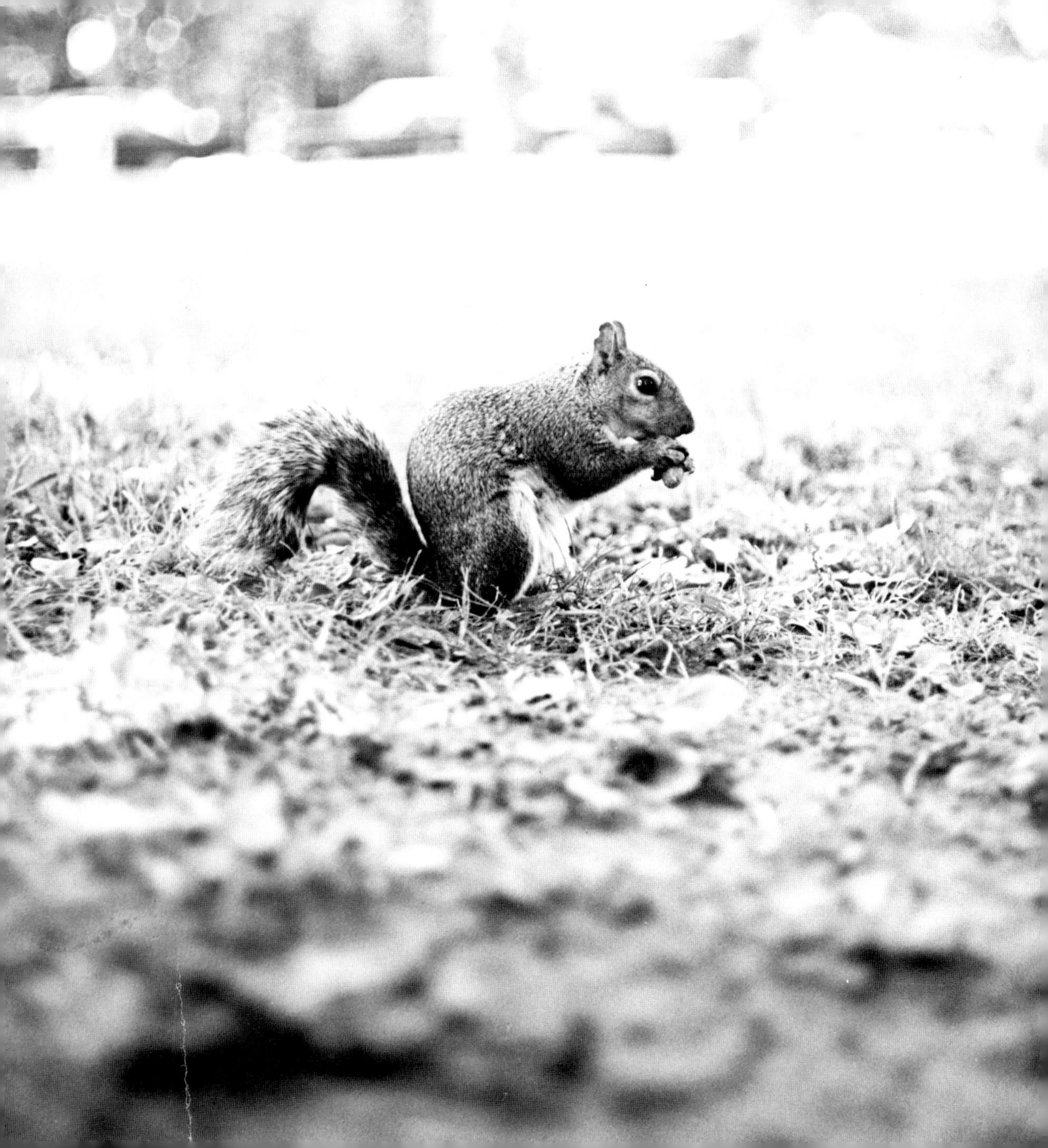

When each living thing has what it needs to live and grow, then the environment is said to be *balanced*. A balanced environment is clean and beautiful. Nothing in it is wasted or unused.

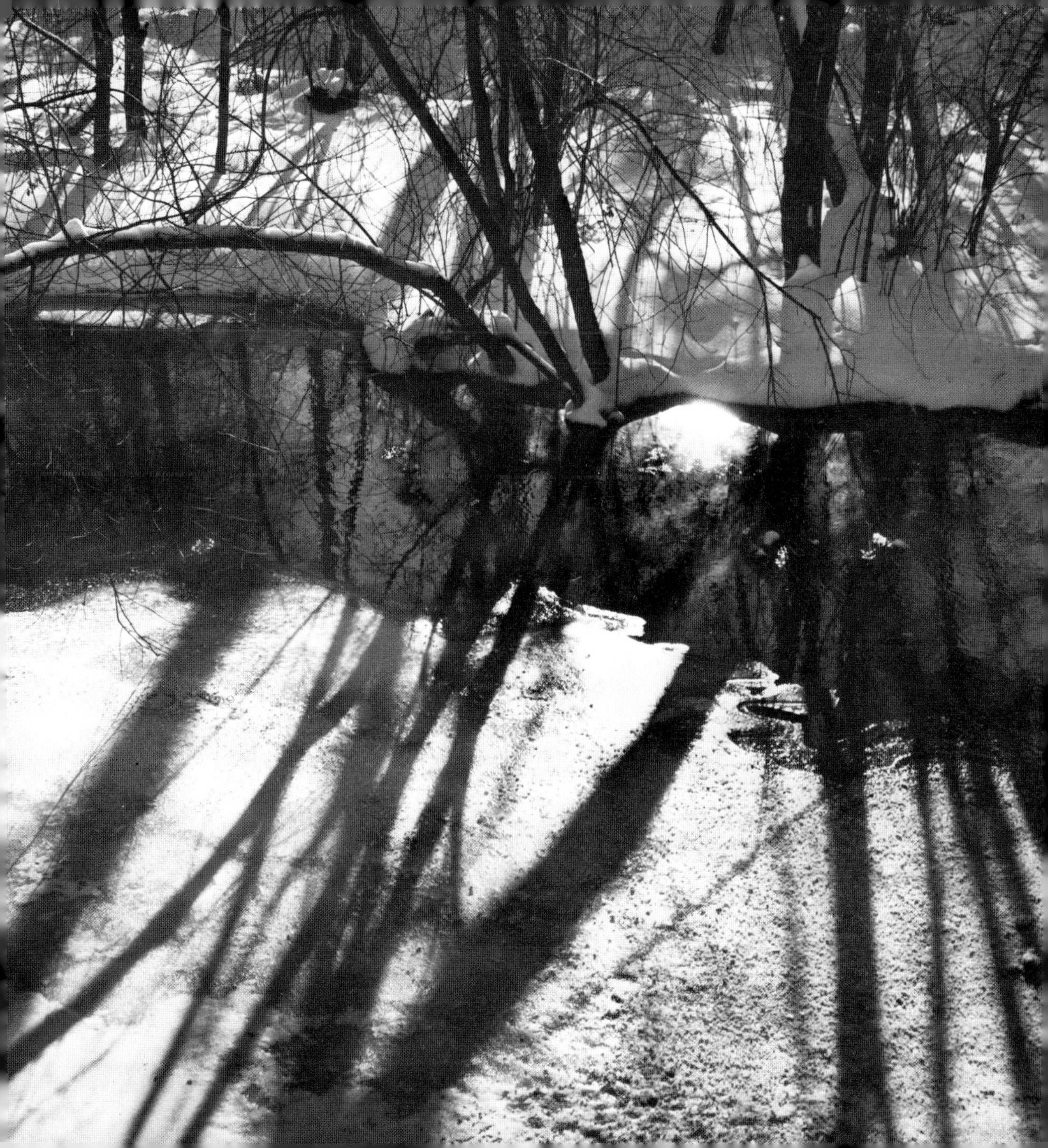

A city environment is very different from a balanced natural environment. In a large city, buildings made of metal and glass stand where trees used to grow, and highways cover the ground. Objects of art help to make up for natural beauty that is lost.

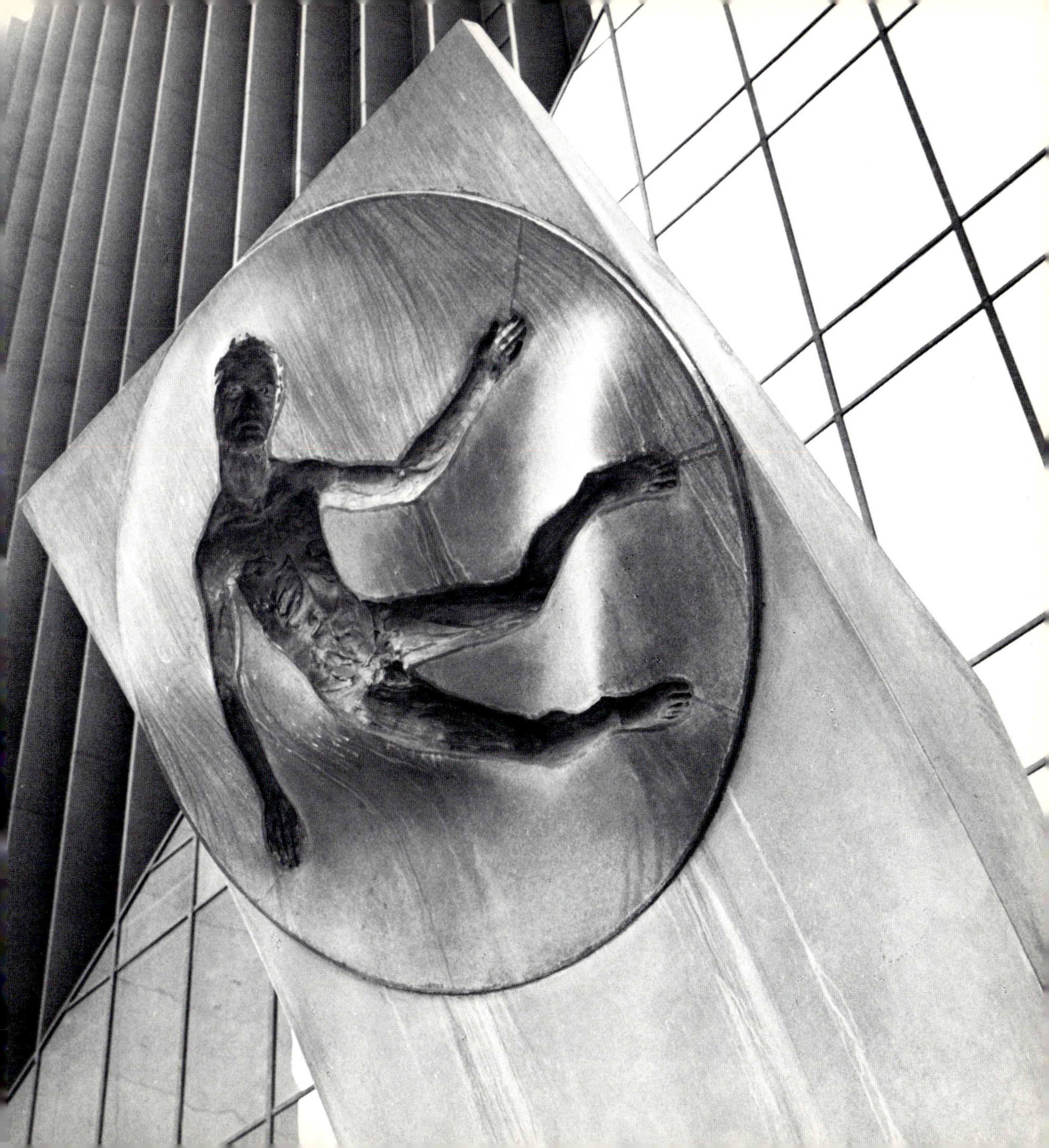

Because the environment of a city is not natural but created by people, it has special kinds of problems.

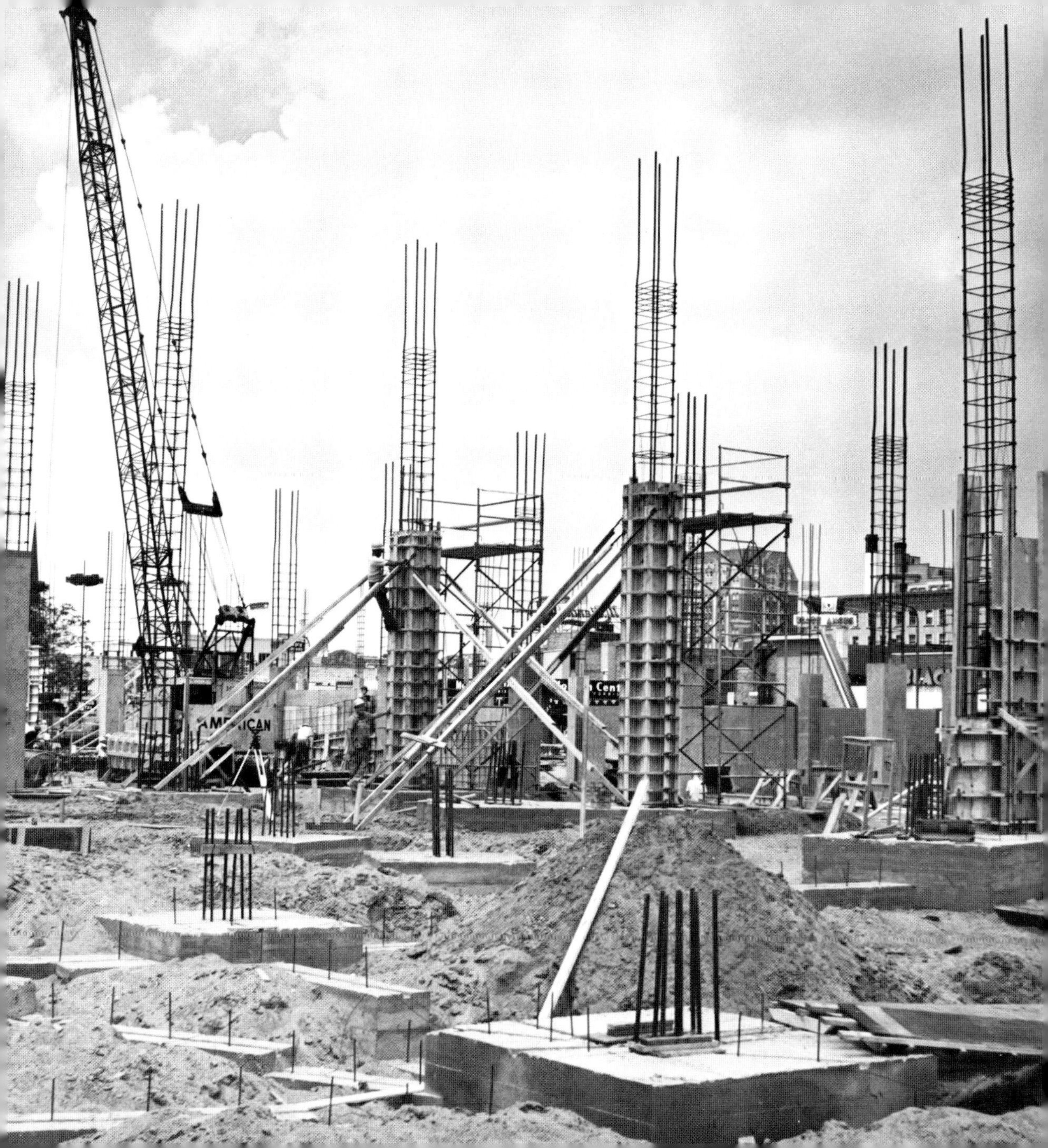
AMERICAN

Some of these problems are caused by our modern way of living. The air in our cities has become filled with the exhaust of automobiles. Rivers and streams are being polluted by the waste products of industry.

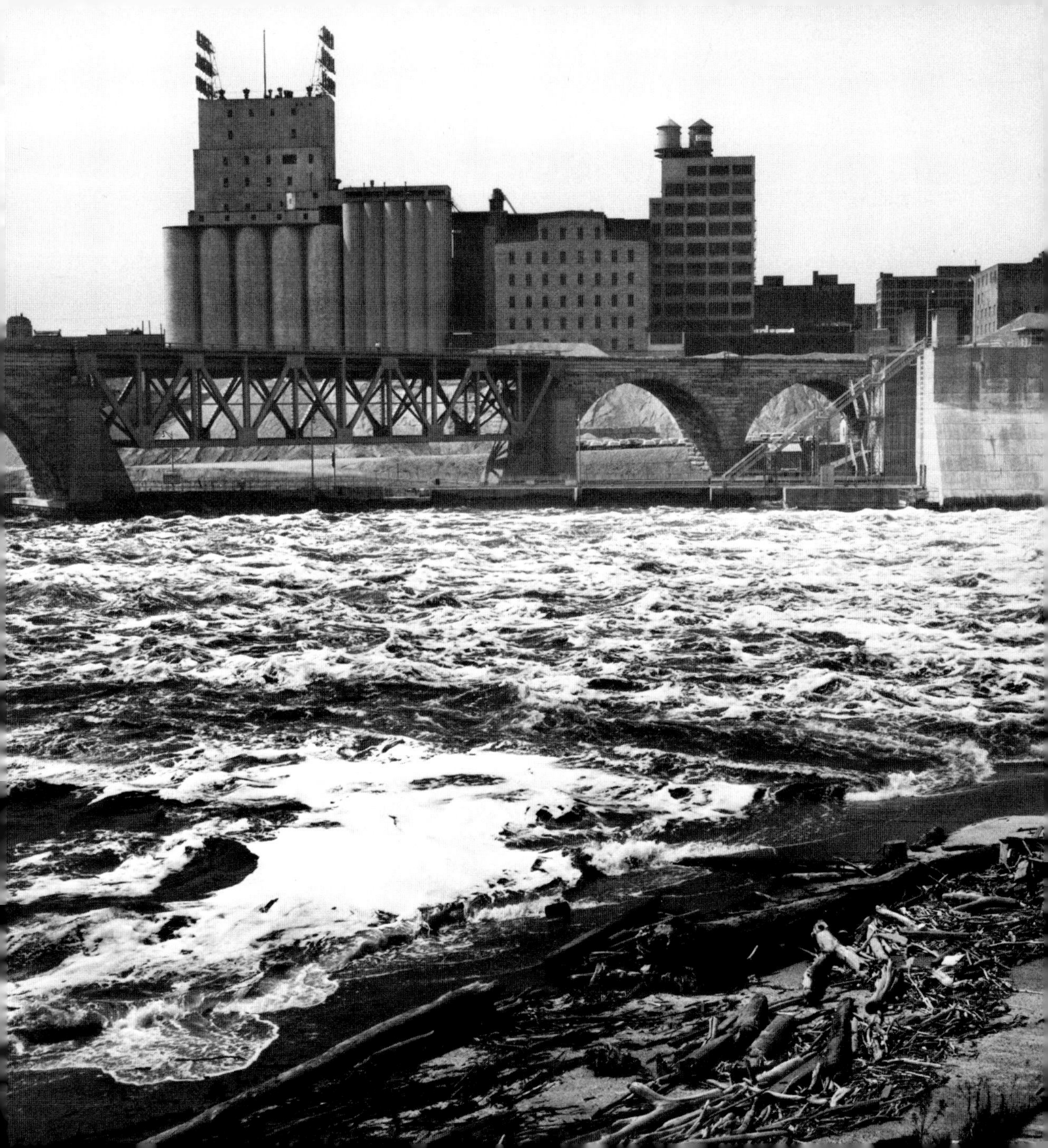

Other problems in a city are caused by overcrowding. With so many people living close together, there is little room to create a pleasant environment.

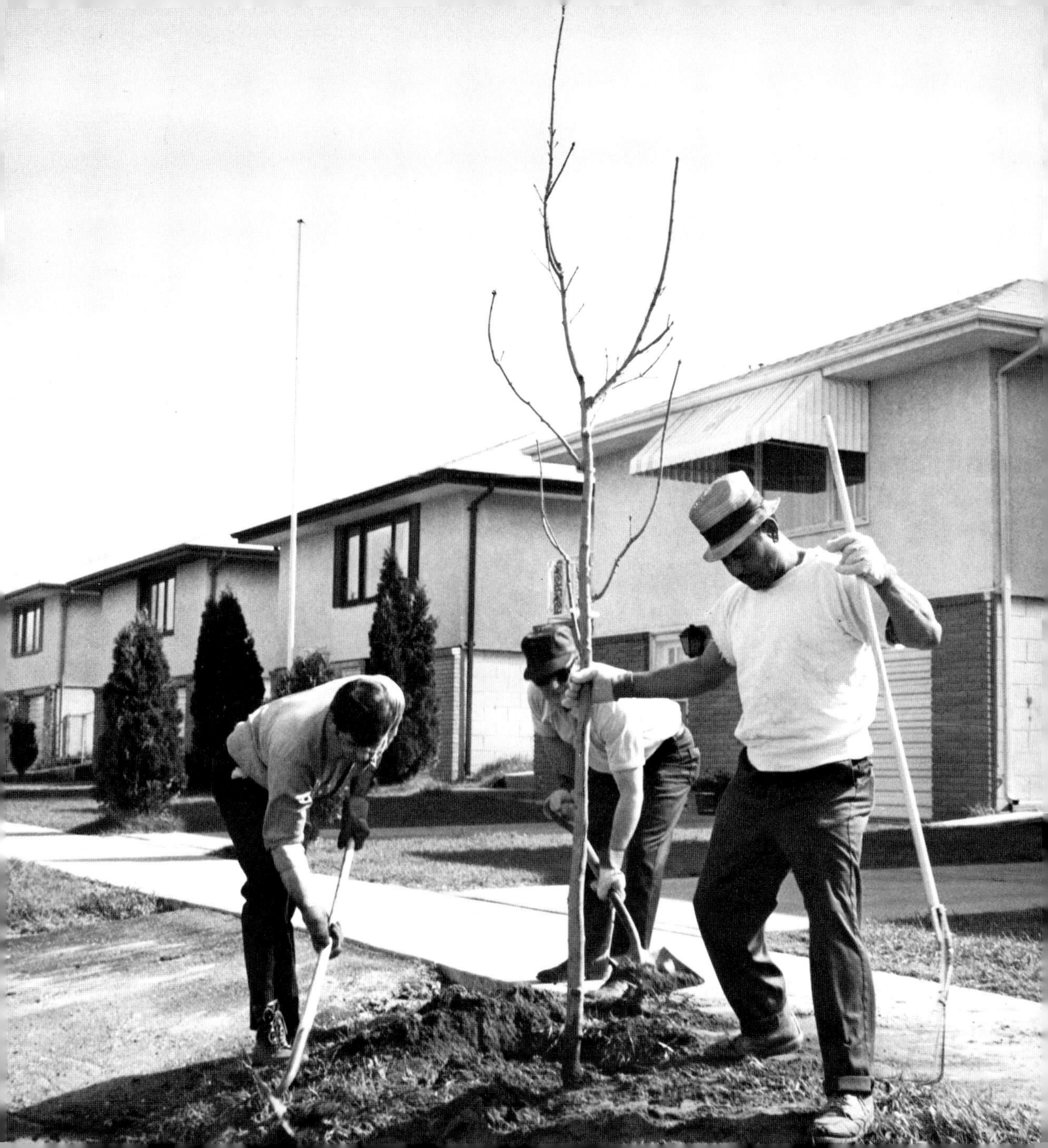

Beyond the city, the environment is also affected by people. As the human population continues to grow, people take more and more from the earth. Plants, animals, and other natural resources are being used faster than they can be replaced.

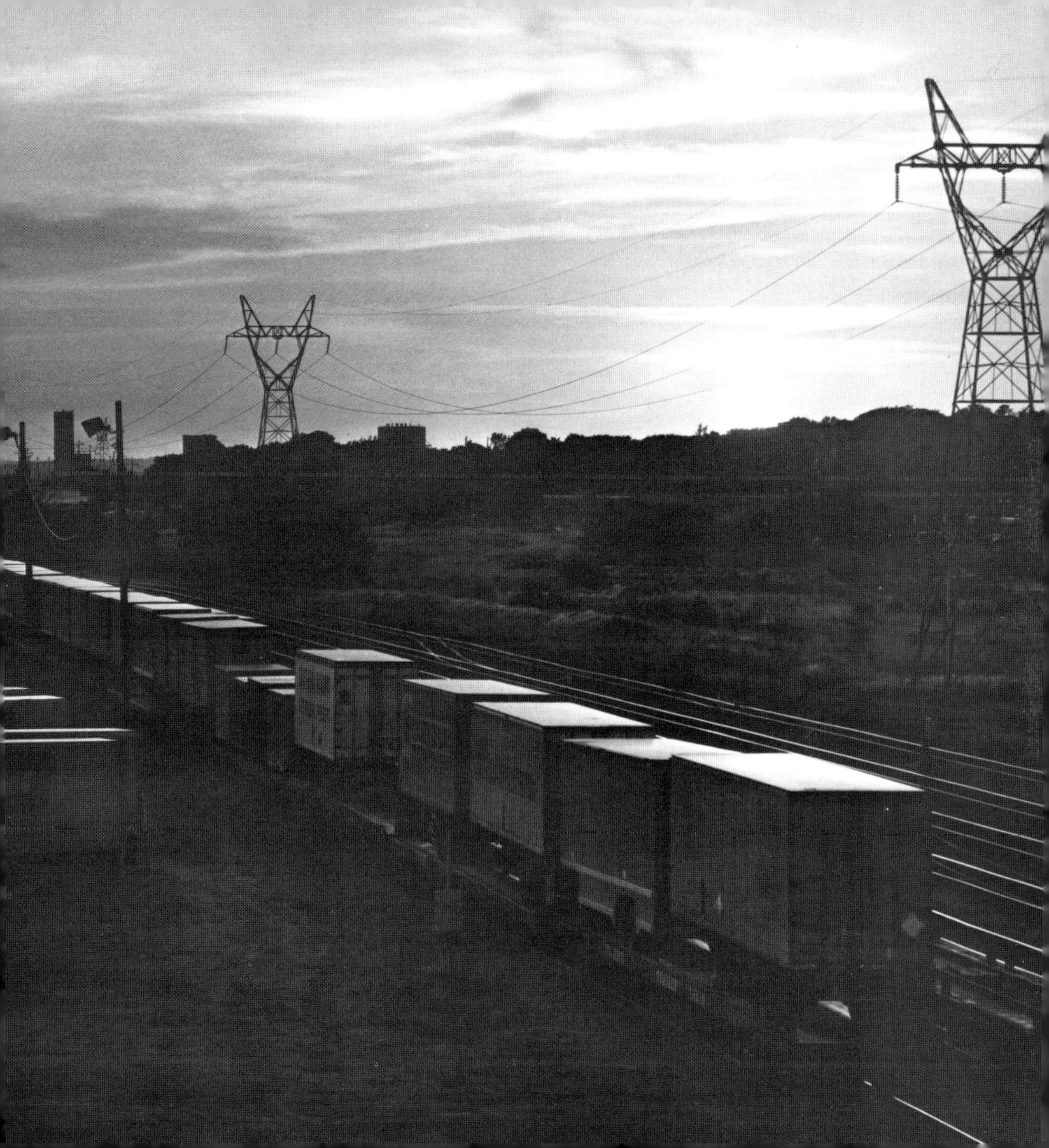

As a result, the delicate balance of the environment has been disturbed.

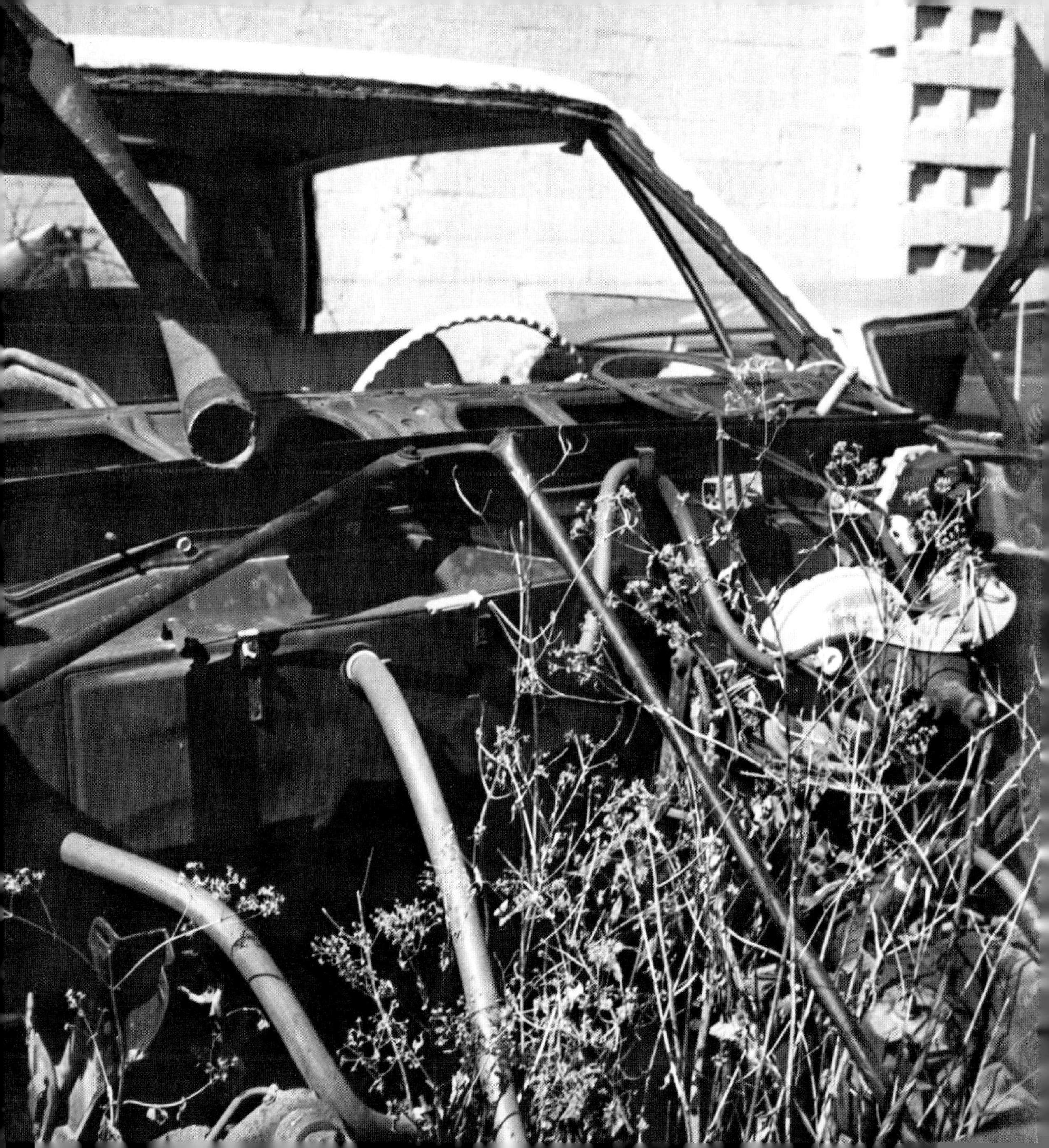

Protecting and taking care of the environment is not an easy job. But with planning and hard work, environmental problems can be solved.

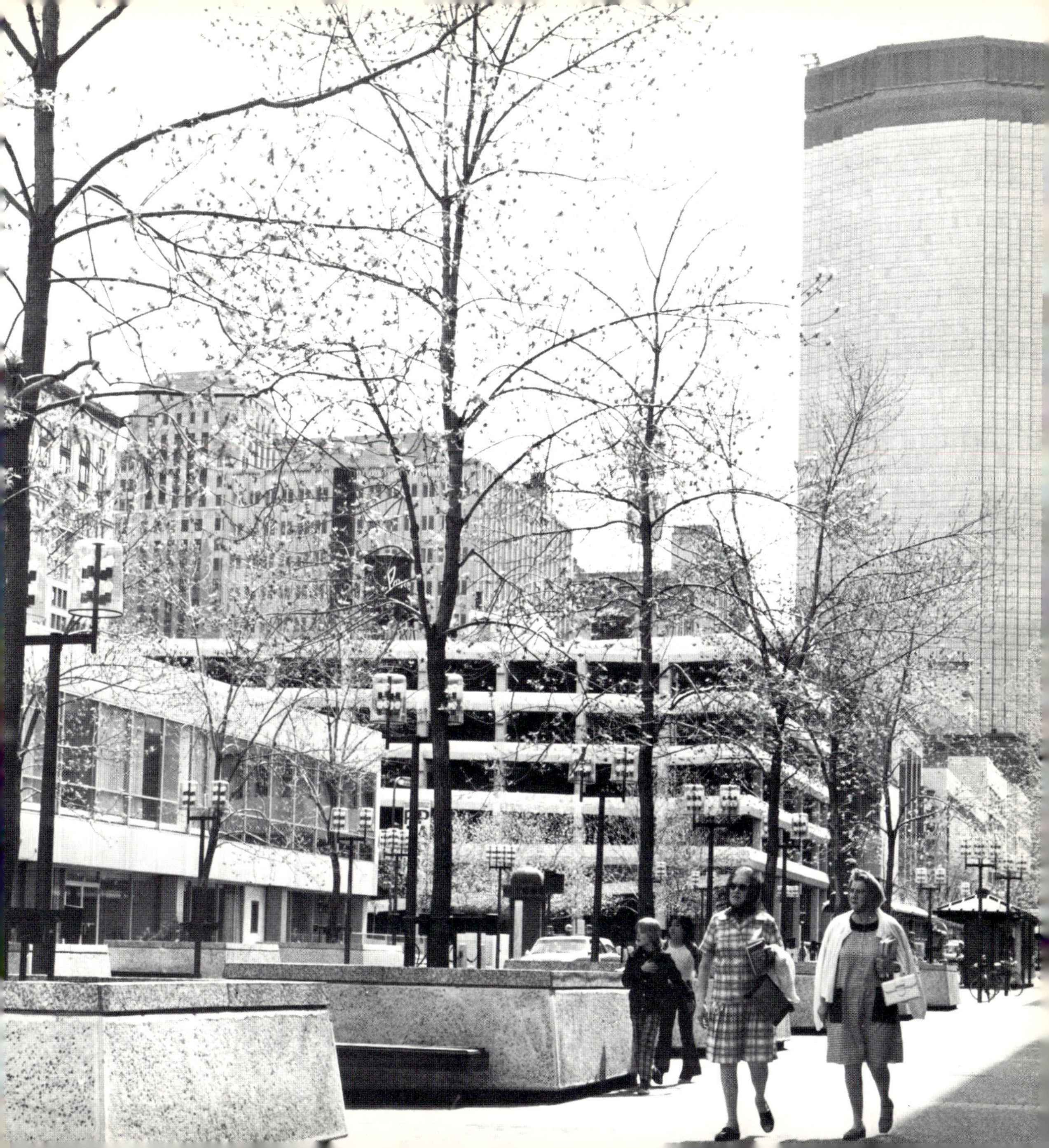

Scientists can find new ways to keep the air and water pure. And elected officials can make laws that prevent industry from polluting the environment.

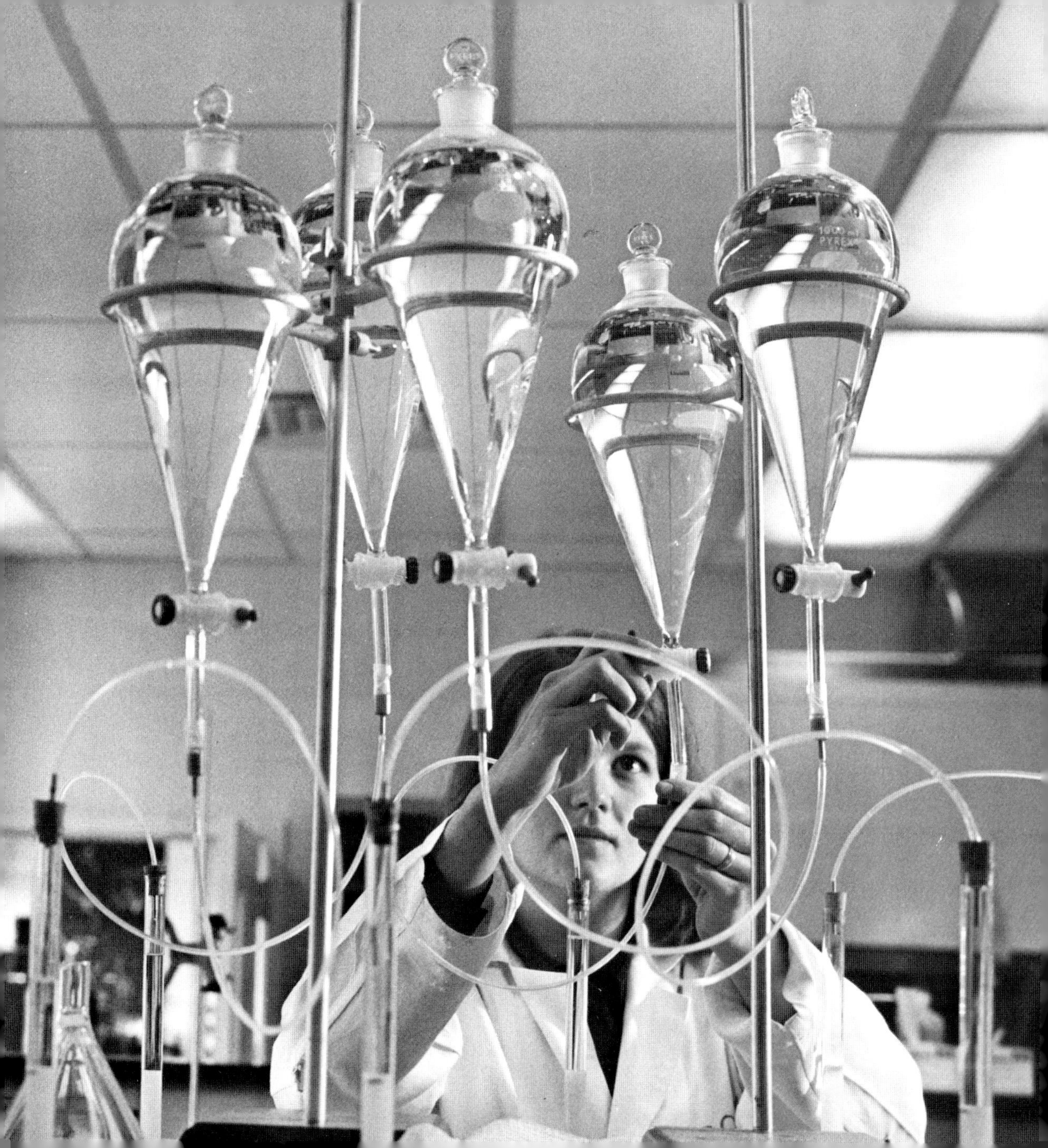

People can begin to have smaller families. Limited population growth will mean a better life for everyone.

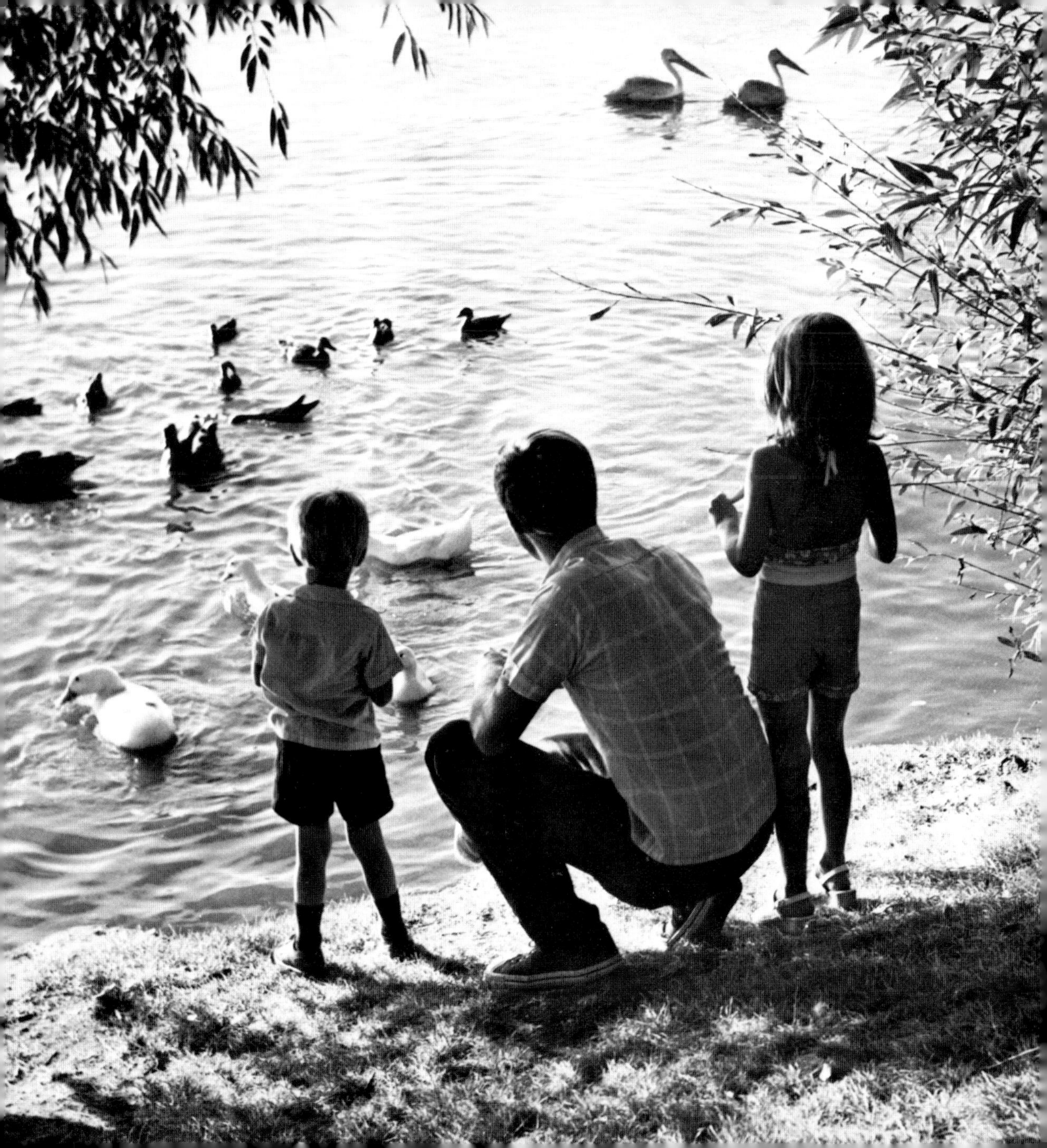

With fewer people making demands on the environment, wildlife and other natural resources will be restored to their natural balance.

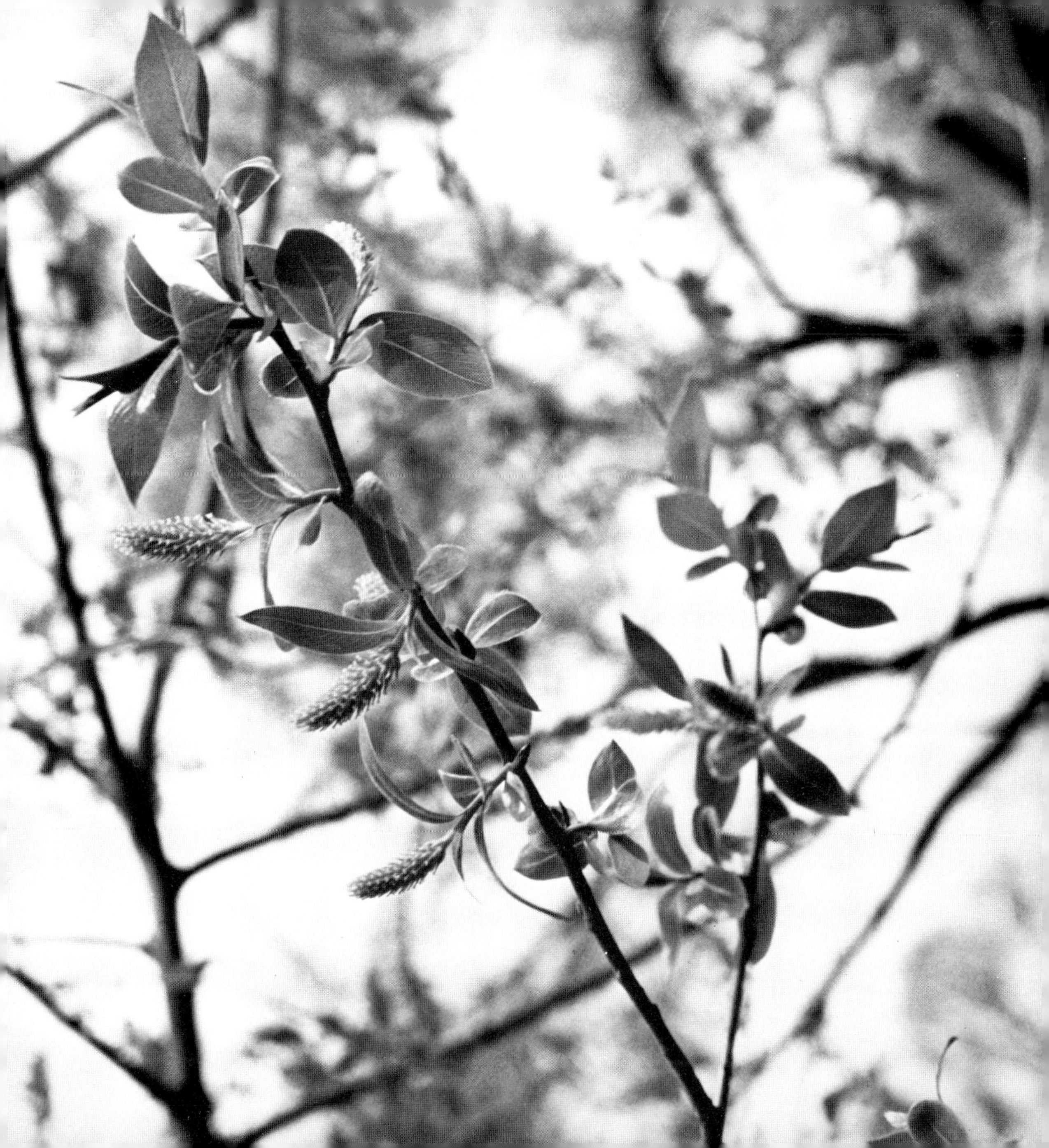

Taking care of the environment is a responsibility that everyone shares. By working together, people can protect the environment and keep it clean and beautiful.

About the Artist

Maria S. Forrai makes her living by taking photographs. "Photography is a family tradition with me," she explains. "In Hungary, where I was born, my mother became a very good portrait photographer. And here in the United States, my husband and I are establishing ourselves as architectural photographers. Designers and builders hire us to take dramatic pictures of their schools, shopping centers, and office buildings." In addition to the work she does with her husband, Maria likes to photograph people. "I try to show the reality of people's lives in my photographs," says Maria. "I want to capture what they are thinking and feeling."

Many of Maria's photographs have won prizes. They have been on display in Leipzig, Germany, as well as in Budapest, Hungary. More recently, her work has been shown at the University of Illinois and at the University of Minnesota. Maria lives with her husband and two children in St. Paul, Minnesota.

301.31 Forrai, Maria S.
FO
    A look at the
      environment

DATE			

HAMILTON MEDIA CENTER
4119 DUPONT AVE. NO.
MINNEAPOLIS, MN 55412

© THE BAKER & TAYLOR CO.